I0449591

The Voice Of LGBT+ Youth In The USA

A huge thanks to everyone who has shared their views and experiences within this book!

Note: Everything you read in this book has come from the views of LGBT+ youth; nothing can be said to be 100% fact.

Contents

How LGBT+ friendly is society?

"It depends on where you live how friendly society is towards LGBT+ people. I live in Alabama so people are very bigoted and unaccepting most of the time, but in places like Colorado and Canada, it isn't near as bad. I have gotten death threats for being trans and have been told multiple times that I'm not, so I wouldn't say it's very accepting where I am."

Landon (he/him), 13, Alabama, demiromantic gynedemisexual, FTM

"In my opinion, society is not very LGBTQ+ friendly depending on where you live; in some places it is illegal, and in others it is punished by death. Some people themselves are more supportive than others, but society itself is not super supportive of it, as they call it a sin…"

Katie (any pronouns), 13, Connecticut, bisexual, genderfluid

"Growing up in a homophobic family, I do know we, as a society, still have a long way to go, but we have made significant improvements in being more accepting of same-sex marriage and trying harder to understand trans people. There are so many kind and friendly people in the world that most take for granted and only focus on the bad. But, I also can't ignore them either because we know there are still unaccepting people. So, all in all, society is not just friendly, but on the other hand, it's not all unaccepting."

Faith (they/them), 14, Kentucky, unsure, non-binary

"I personally believe myself that LGBT+ deserve to be treated like the humans they are and shouldn't have to fear walking out in the world with their loved one. I myself am tired of that fear."

Debra (she/them), 14, Georgia, pansexual & demisexual, non-binary

"I see a lot of hate in the community against bisexuals and asexuals, also there are a lot of (as an example) gay guys invalidating other gay guys for dating a transguy. The community, in my opinion, is not *friendly because of all the gays and lesbians refusing to date bisexuals because 'they have to choose' or invalidating asexuals because 'they haven't found the right person yet'."*

Eliyah (he/him), 16, Texas, asexual, transguy

"No, society as a whole is not LGBT+ friendly. Parts of it are but most aren't. We live in a society that still thinks it's okay not to call someone by their right name or pronouns. It takes seconds to do so, by the way. People purposely call people the wrong name or gender just to hurt them. People think it's okay to physically harm someone who likes the same gender or doesn't conform to the gender norm.

Where homophobia runs rampant throughout kids and adults alike.

It takes less time to just keep quiet and not tear LGBT+ people down than it does to throw insults or worse, punches at them. Society isn't friendly to LGBT+ people unless it can make them the butt of a joke and I hope that one day that can change for the better. Love is love and let people be them."

Gray (they/them), 17, Virginia, bisexual, agender

"Well, in my community, people don't care what you are. If you're nice to them, they'll be nice to you. Except some parents, they are very judgemental. But a lot of the kids are pretty nice about it."

PoppyAnn (they/them), 14, New York, gay, genderfluid

"Today in society, almost everybody, older people, just thinks that everyone has to be straight. Nobody can be but their gender and act their gender. But we are so much more than that. And even some kids today get taught that LGBTQ+ is wrong and not allowed. They get taught that we, LGBTQ+, are the bad people here. So they just bully us."

Chloe (she/he), 13, Virginia, straight, genderfluid

"So, I don't think society is LGBT+ friendly. Sure, there's some people who are okay with it, but overall we're not exactly liked. We are just now starting to get support from companies and it mainly gets shot down from non-LGBT+ people. If you even begin to explain non-binary genders, people just go off the wall telling us we're wrong, and that there's no such thing. People refuse service to same-sex couples. People in the LGBT+ community are dying because we are not

accepted. It's not acceptable."

Mooney (they/them), 16, South Carolina, pansexual, gender-neutral

"I live in the south so I hear on the daily how LGBTQ+ people will 'go to hell'. So, where I live, no one is very friendly towards LGBTQ+ peeps."

Max (she/her), 14, Tennessee, panromantic, female

"I have two opinions on this. I think there are a lot of people who think LGBT+ isn't real and that a lot of people are afraid of what they don't understand. My father is homophobic and it's sad to say because I'm bisexual, but I live my life the way I do. But also, there are people who think LGBT+ is amazing and they support it in every way, whether they are in LGBT+ or not.

So I say about half the world is friendly and the other half is not friendly."

Abbi (he/she/they), 16, Ohio, bisexual, female

"I'd say where I live isn't completely friendly to the LGBT+ community, but I'm still very open. I found myself stuck into this depression that I couldn't get out of, not only because hardly anyone accepted me, but because I couldn't accept myself. Now, I don't really care what anyone thinks. You get to a point in your life when you're ready to be happy and F anyone who tries to ruin that for you."

Grace (she/her), 16, Ohio, lesbian, female

"Society, in some ways, is friendly to the LGBT+ community. Everyone is slightly opening up to being okay with same-sex marriage. But, there are always the people who ban things for us. For example, America just gained a new president around two years ago. He has banned trans people using their bathrooms, LGBT+ people can't get certain jobs because of it, but the thing that gets us all angry is that same-sex marriage is still here. I'm not so sure about the other countries, but I'm sure they're not getting treated right either.

We all want to put a stop to it now. We love the same sex, why is it bothering you? Because it's not in the Bible or it's something that's disgusting? Hate to tell you, but love is love and love wins. People are going to be gay, get over it."

Alex (he/she/they), 15, Maryland, lesbian, genderfluid

"Most people I know are LGBT+ friendly, but I do know that there is a huge part of the population that is not. Heck, my own stepdad, who is very inclusive and supportive (my aunt/his sister has a wife), refuses to refer to ANYONE using they/them pronouns. Support of our community is growing like crazy, and that is absolutely amazing, but its tough when people in our own community do not accept other LGBT+ people. For example, I've heard of many non-straight people who are transphobic.

I think that the rifts in our own community need to be solved before we can get the total support of the society around us."

London (she/they), 13, Washington, panromantic demisexual, girlflux

"It is a very safe place to be in, in this day and age. The LGBTQ+ community has definitely developed throughout the years and has become something great. It doesn't matter what you are because, in this

society, you're mostly accepted. Although there are many people who are homophobic, there are also allies that support our community. Even if you're not accepted where you're from, you're accepted in society, and even today's society is starting to realize it too."

Nat (they/them), 14, California, bisexual, genderfluid

"The LGBT+ is an amazing community and some of the society should understand that. Some do and some don't, but I think that we are who we are and love always wins."

Kim (they/them), 13, Texas, pansexual, agender

"I think society is getting a lot more supportive and accepting of people in the LGBTQ+ community. I see lots of people who treat people of the LGBTQ+ community just like anyone else, which is great. But, as we all know, there are a lot of people in society who are against it or don't understand the community, unfortunately. And it sucks that society can be so accepting yet unaccepting at the same time. But, society is getting a lot more LGBTQ+ friendly. So, society is pretty LGBTQ+ friendly and I hope society

continues to improve and become more friendly."

Elizabeth (she/her), 13, Florida, panromantic & asexual, female

"I am currently only 14 years old and bisexual. Yes I'm young, but I've been around long enough to see that many don't like the LGBT+ community. I think that everyone only focuses on the negative when it comes to this topic, but on a positive note, more and more, year by year, people have been starting to accept the LGBT+ community.

I think that, now, parents talk about the LGBT+ community instead of trying to hide it from their children. It's honestly great I don't feel I have to hide anymore. I actually came out to my best friend today and I'm not scared I won't be accepted. I feel it might not be something every straight teenager is used to, being surrounded by more and more LGBT+ people every year… but more people are accepting us and that's huge!"

Eva (she/her), 14, Illinois, bisexual, female

"Well, I believe the LGBT+ community is here to help

people know that even if you're different, we will accept. We never used to get the rights to marry one another because society felt like that was gross, but now some people have to accept the fact that there are gays, lesbians, bisexuals in the world. The LGBT+ community is a safe place for everyone, even if you're not in it but at least support it."

Chelsey (she/her), 13, Florida, bisexual, female

"A lot of people say the LGBT+ community is a 'disgrace to society' or some say it's wrong, but in reality it's more of a blessing. It shows that love is love no matter the gender.

Some people say they feel bad for the LGBT+ community because we were born that way. While I do believe this is true, I don't regret being pansexual, I don't regret being a bigender MTF trans person. I'm human and I'm ME and that's not something I regret. I love being who I am and I never wish I was different, because if I was, I wouldn't be me."

Nix (she/her), 15, South Carolina, pansexual, bigender MTF

"I live in California, which is a very liberal state. This, I hoped, would mean less homophobes and transphobes than other places. I was correct in the way that homophobes and transphobes weren't physical in their harassment, but comments were still thrown around and I was still subjected to verbal harassment, mostly comments not directed at me, but still painful. This has prevented me from coming out."

Gem (she/her), 14, California, pan, demigirl

"Society is not very friendly because a lot of people are very homophobic, and I think it's stupid and people should just accept people for the way they are. Also, a lot of people are killing themselves because they're getting bullied or they're getting threats from people."

Brandy (he/him), 13, North Carolina, ace, guy

"Overall, the society isn't very kind to the LGBT+ community. Society teaches kids that being LGBT+ is unnatural, and even treats it like a curse word. Still, about 168 out of 195 countries don't allow same-sex marriage! But, on the other hand, a growing number of countries are allowing it. Sadly, even when all of the

world normalizes the LGBT+ community, there's always going to be homophobes and transphobes no matter what."

Mary (she/her), 12, Ohio, omnisexual, female (cis)

"Society isn't that LGBT+ friendly all in all, but sometimes there are places and there are people who are kind enough to think about the feelings of others. Society is much more friendly to LGBT+ people now than before, and I'm out to a lot of people, but it's taken a lot of work to get there. The world as a whole is not entirely LGBT+ friendly, and until we manage to get there, there's a lot more fighting to be done."

Wynn (he/him), 14, Illinois, aromantic asexual, male

In what ways could society be improved for members of the LGBT+ community?

"Honestly, the main way society can be improved is just by going forward and not looking back. No more backwards laws against the LGBTQ+ community, only progressive laws that make it so everyone can feel and be equal."

Esmée (she/her), 16, USA, pan, trans

"I believe society could, of course, accept anyone who wants to truly be happy and in order for people to be happy, they have to become what they wish and what they feel. Society is focused too much on what people SHOULD be in their eyes and that, in my opinion, is wrong and not welcoming. The LGBT+ community deserves much better than that, considering the big change we had to go through to realize who we are today. And that, my friend, is a hard process."

Max/Maxine (no pronouns), 15, Texas, pansexual, female

"I don't know how to put it but we could always come out, and not hesitate to do anything. Let us be us. I feel like we should do more to make the president notice and let us marry who we want!"

Elyse (they/them), 15, Nebraska, bisexual, agender

"I just feel like we in the LGBT+ community are not accepted as much as people say we are. It's just insulting to have people accept you, but then when someone asks about you, they go off and say that they don't accept us. And I feel like there needs to be more support for the LGBT+ community. More than there is now.

People say, 'You don't feel safe or comfortable here? Well go to the school guidance counsellor'. But most of the time, they make things worse. And the so-called 'safe spaces' don't really help anyone. And just because someone is gay, trans etc. doesn't mean they wanna be your 'gay best friend' or 'special friend'."

Alex (he/him), 16, Rhode Island, gay, trans

"I feel that society shouldn't criminalize LGBT+ people

just for liking the same gender, not being straight or being LGBT+ in general and start actually looking at people for who they are, not who they aren't."

Jay (he/they), 17, Maryland, pansexual, FTM

"Society could be improved for members of the LGBT+ community in many ways, such as not refusing service to a person due to their sexuality or their gender identity. Society could help normalize it, instead of always tending to make a big deal out of it. With more serious cases of harsher punishment for being LGBT+, they could stop seeing through eyes full of nothing but hate. Stop treating it as something poisonous, when it's just people trying to be who they are and love who they love."

Andrew (he/him), 15, Washington, pansexual, male

"I feel that society should be more accepting so that people in the community, still in the closet or not, feel more comfortable being who they are."

Reese (she/her), 15, Texas, lesbian, female

"A way society could improve is definitely how gays and straights get along. Like, there's a million straight icons and maybe two gay ones, but then straights are always like, 'Why does everything have to be gay?' and gays come back with, 'Why does everything have to be straight?'. My thing is, why can't everything just be about love? And it not matter about gender?"

Eron (they/she/any), 16, Georgia, gay, genderfluid

"More representation in media would help LGBTQ+ people. Straight and cis people that openly advocate the LGBTQ+ community would also help. Education about queer history in schools would help eliminate a lot of homophobia and transphobia.

Following the philosophy of Harvey Milk, if you come out to people, they are less likely to be scared of gay people. If they are told that gay people are bad or are never really talked to about it, they're most likely going to fear people who are different from them. However, it is a lot harder to hate somebody that you know or a friend even.

I remember growing up and until age 9 I didn't even know what gay meant and I thought that 'lesbian' was a bad word. At age 9, my dad talked to me about it and said that some people are gay. I asked what that meant and he said, 'It's when a man loves a man or when a woman loves a woman'."

Eli (they/them), 14, New York, asexual, non-binary

"I think that in all schools there should be some sort of safe space for kids who feel uncomfortable or are being bullied. I also think that public places should have bathrooms for anyone who feels uncomfortable going into a female or male restroom."

Willow (she/her), 13, Illinois, lesbian, female

"I think it could be improved a lot by churches who accept LGBT+ people, and letting two boys go to prom with each other. Giving us human rights. Not 'gay rights'. I think we should make being LGBT+ our new normal. Oh, you're gay? That's great. You're a trans guy? You look handsome. Be proud, not ashamed."

Jace (he/him), 15, Minnesota, pansexual, boy

"Society could keep their thoughts to themselves

instead of telling us we are worthless and we should go kill ourselves. They could just keep it to themselves. I'm scared to come out to the whole world because I think people will bully me, or hurt me for being who I am."

Brooklyn (he/she/they), 12, California, acesexual panromantic, other

"For the LGBTQ+ community, there has always been issues, fighting, and hate, all because people want to love who they want to love. It's funny how this is all caused by people who don't like the thought of people not being straight.

What could society do to be improved for the LGBTQ+ community? Society can go s**** themselves. Like. Seriously? Hundreds of teens commit suicide/hurt themselves every single day because society can't bare the thought of someone being who they were born to be. Most of us are even afraid to leave our houses and go to school, where we have a s***** time already because other teens are taught that not being straight is a bad thing, and we have to take it all. All because we are who we were born as.

*So what can society do to help the LGBTQ+
community? P*** off."*

Emma (she/her), 14, USA, bi, cisgender (female)

*"If people didn't shame them or use 'gay' as an insult.
If people would accept them or just keep their mouths
shut. If people would treat LGBT+ people normally,
and not like aliens."*

Blake (she/her), 13, Wisconsin, pansexual, cis girl

*"I think that society should have more safe places for
people like us. I also think that society needs to put in
more bathrooms that are safe for LGBTQ+. Society
should also stop acting like we are some type of
horrid thing that kills you."*

A.J (she/they), 15, North Carolina, gay, female

*"Society can be improved for LGBT+ members by
teaching kids at a younger age some respect for
them! Like, have some classes in school for it. I think
a good idea would be schools for just LGBT+
members so they can be out and not worry about*

getting bullied at school. It might not happen but I think it's a good idea. Also, some summer camps for members of the LGBT+ community where they can just have a nice queer summer! That would be nice."

Kya (she/her), 13, USA, unsure, female

"Society could definitely improve a lot of things for the LGBTQ+ community. I mean, for starters, they could stop treating us like we're not human. If they would just accept us more, things would be so much better. Nobody should be denied basic human rights because of who they love. I will be glad the day this country changes how they view the LGBTQ+ community and hope I live to see it."

Miya (she/her), 14, US, pansexual, female

"Society can improve in so many ways to make members of the LGBT+ community more comfortable and equal. The government needs to stop discriminating against us and set down basic laws to make us equal. Like, allowing transgender members into the military and not have a transgender bathroom ban. The citizens of society need to be taught about our community and not to fear/hate us, but to accept

us as human beings just like them. They can also not make it harder for members of the LGBT+ community to adopt children.

Everyone should be equal and accepted no matter who you are. Society should love (accept and make us equal to them) rather than fear us. Once you get to know the LGBT+ community, we can be a lot of fun."

Josey (she/her), 15, South Carolina, lesbian, female

How well-educated are people on the LGBT+ community?

"As an individual from a more southern state – Texas to be exact – I did not learn about the LGBT+ community till I was 13. Same goes for other southern states due to their abstract way of thinking about homosexuality. This also goes for homophobic countries that kill homosexuals for 'sport'. The education system usually does not involve a lesson about sexual orientation which usually leaves kids to venture on their own to try to find worthy resources; not to mention most likely reading false information (such as lesbians cannot contract STIs)."

Mady (she/her), 16, Texas, bisexual, female

"I think many people have a good understanding of homosexuality now. Where it gets a little iffy is the understanding and education on other sexualities, such as asexual and bisexual."

Britney (she/her), 18, North Carolina, bisexual, female

"I feel like a lot of community members are very aware of the different aspects of the LGBT+ community and how they work and develop. But there's also a lot in the LGBT+ world that don't know that much and don't really care to know."

Coreanna (she/they), 17, Illinois, bisexual, female mostly

"I feel like people aren't really educated on the LGBT+ community because most of them think that they're the good guys and LGBT+ is evil and it's taking their loved ones away. They just react poorly to things because they're afraid or they don't understand things fully. That creates fear, but it's not really their fault because nobody thinks they're the bad guy of the situation. They were just born a different time period and it's hard to unlearn what they were taught. But overall, I think people should educate themselves before they have a say in the situation."

Guadalupe (any pronouns), 15, Illinois, gay, non-binary

"Well for starters, people shouldn't teach their children that the 'norm' is cisgender boy/girl or that

heterosexuals are the only valid sexuality. Also, homophobics NEED to learn that homophobia doesn't make you hetero (straight)."

Ollie (they/she), 13, California, pansexual, demigirl

"If I'm being honest, no-one is well educated anymore. If you bring any term related to any such subject, they push it aside. Almost like they don't even care, but I bet if they had gotten a better understanding of it then maybe, just maybe, people would understand the community better.

In my honest opinion, I feel like if society had been educated better then there wouldn't be so much hate. If people understood what it was like to walk in any LGBTQ+ person's shoes, they wouldn't be as cruel as they are now.

Society hasn't been educated about anything. Whatever people deem normal, that is what goes. If someone or something is out of place or not what they call normal, they shame them… only because they don't understand them and because they fear that something worse will come out of it. If they knew only just a little more than they hear or think, maybe things would be different…

Maybe then everyone can live together and have a peaceful life, but most people don't see it like that. Most people see it as a 'threat'. I say this because when something or someone seems happy or has a better life, you want to attack that said person or thing. Why? Because you want them to feel like you. Though it's wrong, people still do this. Because if everyone is the same then there is no 'threat', no-one who has anything better. They are just like you.

But so is the community. We are just people trying to get by with life while those around us are not accepting or accepting. It all depends on how one was educated through their life."

Alex (he/him), 15, Florida, pansexual, trans male

"I think people should be more educated on the LGBTQ+ community because we are people too. It will help people understand more and there may be less violence towards us."

Jean (he/him), 17, Florida, questioning, FTM

"Well basically, a lot of people still don't, like, understand most of the labels. A lot of the time when I

come out to people in the community as pansexual non-binary, I get so many questions like, 'Isn't that just bisexual?' or, 'How can you be non-binary? Pick one'. Plus, some people I've talked to don't understand that labels can change because I used to go by bisexual but then I realized pansexual worked better for me. That confused so many people. The main labels I think that people don't understand are aro and ace. A lot of people in the community have no clue how they would work."

Harley (they/them), 17, California, pansexual, non-binary

"Judging from my personal experience, people from outside of the community don't know much about it. Most of the time, people don't understand what being transgender means, what being a lesbian means, what bisexual means, the differences between transgender people and drag queens or crossdressers, the history of homophobic slurs they use or just queer history in general.

There are four churches within 2 miles of each other in my town. It's predominantly white and middle class. All the places of worship in our town are Christian-based, and there are no temples or mosques. On a day-to-day basis, I don't really experience transphobia, people rarely use my birth name but still use my old pronouns.

A lot of my friends are transphobic and don't like non-binary people so I haven't come out to them. They just kind of call me by my name and nothing else. I've tried to explain to one of my friends and he keeps on asking me if I'm actually trans or not. A few years back, it got out that I was trans and everyone was really confused."

Eli (they/them), 14, New York, asexual, non-binary

"In general, I think people know what gay and trans people are. They know of people like Caitlyn Jenner and Neil Patrick Harris. They might know about famous gay people or gay stereotypes but they don't understand beyond that. If they make a little more effort then they know what bisexuality is. They might know that famous people like Miley Cyrus or Demi Lovato are bisexual. They might know what non-binary is and have their own opinion that it's real or not.

Very few people go past the '+' in LGBT+. Those who do probably know about QIA. They know about the

1.5% of people who are intersex (don't quote me on that statistic, I'm not sure if it was correct). They know about asexuality but not aromanticism. A few know about the P for pansexual. It's likely, unless they're in the community, they won't know more. And lastly, I would like to say that the exception to this is book authors. Book authors know everything."

Annabel (she/they), 14, California, omniromantic grey-ace homosexual, demigirl

"Both members and non-members of the LGBT+ community are not educated enough about the community. This is partially because of the lack of representation in the media, but also because of stereotypes and untrue rumors."

Fran (she/her), 15, Utah, biromantic asexual, female

"Society is so poorly educated about LGBT+ that a lot of people I've met don't know what bisexual, nonbinary or asexual mean. People could be better educated about it by adding LGBT+ characters to children's stories instead of the forced het romances and the gendered prophecies."

Pete (he/they), 12, Washington DC, pansexual, questioning

"I grew up around the LGBTQ+ community. My sister's best friend was lesbian and now trans, so I was educated from a very young age, but other people don't have experiences like that. They may be very religious or live in a small town and not know LGBTQ+ exists. Some kids are raised to hate because of their parents' beliefs, but I don't think they know enough to even believe them. They say the Bible says it's wrong, but the Bible also says divorce, tattoos, eating pig and rabbit, wearing two different fabrics is wrong.

I think most people are very uneducated. They think it's just a bunch of gays and do not take time to look at everyone in LGBTQ+. I think most people, who are not allies, are uneducated about it."

Morgan (she/her), 14, Ohio, bisexual, female

"It truly depends on the person, who they choose to befriend, and the area in which they live. It also depends on the parents, and whether or not they support the LGBT+ community. It would be nice to

have a greater number of people to be educated on the community, however this is very unlikely considering the fact that many people don't want to learn about subject matters which do not accept them. However, even though people are not well educated on the community, the amount of support is raising."

Emiliano (he/him), 14, Texas, bi, male

Is there enough representation of the LGBT+ community in the media?

"There is not enough representation of LGBT+ in the media. Anybody who's gay in a TV show or movie is the stereotypical gay best friend who loves glitter and sparkles and says stuff like, 'You go girl!!!!'. It's fine if you're gay and you act like that, but not all gay people are like that."

Gia (she/her), 13, California, pansexual, female

"No there isn't. The library at my old town had no books and no movies with LGBT+ characters. Then, after we moved to Jonesboro, my friends and I were going to have an LGBT+ movie night. We looked through the library for two hours and found no movies with LGBT+ characters. When looking for books in this library, there are about ten with LGBT+ characters in a library with thousands of books. I want to see people like me in movies and books."

Jayden (he/him), 16, Arkansas, bisexual, trans man

"I don't really know but in my opinion, there should be more people being able to represent the LGBT+ community on social media. Many people delete their accounts after hate comments. The only representation we've really got is from famous people but in reality, they only post about it when something happens to the community. They don't talk about it ever again.

Many kids don't represent their community because they are not out or someone might stumble upon their account and show their parents. I really don't believe there is enough."

Tyler (he/him), 16, Florida, bisexual, trans

"This is a complicated question. Firstly, there are many groups included in our community, many of which are greatly publicized and well known (such as the most known name of the community 'LGBT'). And secondly, enough is a subjective word. Acknowledging that, we can start to unravel the question.

A large portion of our community is not even known about to those who are less involved; lesser known genders, spectrums of sexualities completely glossed over etc. You cannot generalize this kind of publicity because you would be ignoring the erasure of many, many individuals such as myself who have absolutely no representation.

The other part to this is who sees the representation? Certainly not children of unaccepting families or teenagers without access to things like YouTube. In fact, a very large portion of viewers are haters who turn our representation into something of fear. Some of us hadn't even heard of the community in a positive way until we became adults.

Personally, I think it wouldn't be fair to ask such a general question to such a diverse group. It would be like saying 'Did you receive proper sex education in school?' to groups of both toddlers and adults. It doesn't work because it can't apply to parts of the audience. And so, that is my personal take on the question."

Nick/Elliot (he/they), 13, New York, ace, bigender

"To be honest, I think there's a pretty good amount of people I know personally and who I follow who are a part of LGBT+. Even if they aren't LGBT+, they still support the community. So in my opinion, I think there

is."

Cienna (she/he), 16, North Carolina, pansexual, female/genderfluid

"There's too much at this point. People are shoehorning in LGBTQ+ characters for the sake of appealing to us. They add nothing to the overall arc other than, 'Hey, we have a gay character, you can't hate us now', and I'm sick of it. They need to stop cramming gay characters into good shows for the sake of having a gay character."

Adalyn (she/her), 16, Ohio, straight ally, female

"I don't think we do. There is so much negative representation of us that it's tainting how people view us. I think what we need is more positive representation by LGBT+ people who accept all genders and sexualities, not just the ones they are and a few others."

Destiny (she/they), 14, Minnesota, pansexual, genderfluid

"There definitely isn't enough LGBTQ+ representation in the media. Looking at the statistics, the total amount of queer people in media doesn't reflect the actual population. This means there is an under-representation. Having more queer representation in media would be positive for queer youth. Seeing those like themselves on TV shows or in movies for minorities makes them feel less alone and characters could easily serve as positive role models.

The representation we get currently is subpar; gay characters end up getting killed a lot or are side characters, such as in The Walking Dead."

Eli (they/them), 14, New York, asexual, non-binary

"I don't think there is because it's always shown on TV as cis-straight people. When there is an LGBT+ person, they aren't a main character and they aren't talked about as important in anything."

Kayden (she/they/he), 12, Oregon, pansexual, genderfluid

"I don't think that there is enough LGBT+ representation in media, specifically in children's

media. *Though there are a few exceptions, children's media often portrays many of their characters (on a show/movie/book) as heterosexual.*

In media marketed towards adolescents, LGBT+ people are portrayed fairly well. There are still many books with solely heterosexual characters. However, many authors are adding LGBT+ characters to their YA novels, which is an improvement from the past. It's often overlooked as well.

Lastly, in adult media, LGBT+ people are portrayed a bit less frequently than in adolescent culture, which is likely purposeful. Authors and directors understand what their audiences want. If LGBT+ teens are now the majority, more YA novels will come out with LGBT+ characters. If LGBT+ adults still make up 10% of the adult population, so be it. Adult media won't show as many LGBT+ people.

And children's media is likely only using heterosexual characters because they understand that if they had a gay character, the show's ratings would go down."

Sophia (she/her), 14, Georgia, lesbian, female

"We've been seeing some representation of our

community lately, and we know how important it is to have that in the media. We think what's going on right now is great, but we still have some ceilings to break before we can truly be integrated into this society as normal. I think it'd be ideal if we shine more light down on those who have suffered from being who they are to spread awareness and welcome everyone as a member of our nation."

Jessie (they/them), 16, New York, pan, genderfluid

"Of course, yes there is a lot of representation at present in all media. It's a very good thing thanks to the fact that people can express themselves with freedom."

Karina (no pronouns), 18, California, lesbian, female

"I feel like there is LGBT+ representation in the media. That doesn't mean it's enough or even good representation. In recent years, there have been improvements. I've seen non-stereotypical gay couples in cartoons.

Sometimes, I feel like there's a progression to representation. It goes: stereotypical LGBT+ white person; non-stereotypical LGBT+ white person; non-stereotypical LGBT+ POC. Repeat process until we've got the representation we need and deserve.

I'd rather have good representation of the whole community right now. However, I doubt cis-het people would accept that. So, I suppose, we can work towards our goal slowly. We'll get there eventually."

Abby (any pronouns), 14, Illinois, panromantic asexual, cis girl

"There isn't enough representation in the media. While they've finally started having gay and lesbian characters in TV etc., the rest of the community is never acknowledged, such as asexuals, non-binary genders, and basically every gender and sexuality that isn't part of the 'LGBT' acronym."

Jordan (they/she), 15, California, pansexual/lesbian, non-binary/questioning

"No, there is not enough representation of the LGBT+ community in the media. In the shows I watch, when or even if there are any LGBT+ characters, there are bad stereotypes that are used when portraying the

character.

Most LGBT+ teens struggle with coming to terms with who they are, and not having anyone to relate to on such a popular platform adds to that struggle. Maybe it's just me but having someone to relate to and showing you that you're not a freak helps not to feel alone.

If there was more representation of the LGBT+ community when I was younger, I probably would have accepted and loved myself for who I am earlier."

Ashton (they/them), 17, North Carolina, pansexual, genderfluid

"Currently, there is nowhere near enough representation in the media for the LGBT+ people. When I was young, I thought I was messed up, or that I was crazy for not wanting to be a girl. I never even knew transgender was a thing until I was around 12. I didn't even know girls could kiss, date, or get married.

Homophobic and transphobic people think we don't need anything at all, or that the TV shows and movies are unrealistic with how many LGBT+ characters are in them. Most of today's teens are LGBT+ in one form

of another. It's no longer uncommon for someone to be bi, gay, or trans. We need kids to know they're okay, they're not going crazy."

Emerson (he/him), 14, Pennsylvania, pansexual, FTM

"No, there isn't enough representation in the media. In recent years, there has been more with LGBT+ stars, such as Miles McKenna, and movies, such as Love, Simon. But with most media with queer characters, it is centered around their queerness, and biases. I want to read a story where there's a queer person who fights a monster, goes in a spaceship, or something where being queer isn't a problem. I'm not saying books centered around oppression are bad, I'm just saying more representation is needed."

Amelia (they/them), 14, Wisconsin, pansexual, non-binary

"I feel like there is a lot of representation of LGBTQ+ on social media, but not enough. Equality is a HUGE problem right now, and social media is helping and hurting at the same time. I mean, you have people like Hayley Kiyoko and Thomas Sanders who are very open about their sexuality on social media and

are helping a lot. However, this will not change the world many people see us in.

Some of us feel hidden, stuck in a world where no one loves us, and social media is an escape. This is where all the LGBTQ+ accounts come in. We represent us in a very open way, but even with all of us, there's an equal or greater amount of people who see life in a different way, a homophobic way. They represent most of society, which is sad, but true. They are what most people see when they go online.

I have had my Instagram account for two days and have already had someone send me Bible quotes and say, 'You're going to hell'. This is not ok. We need more people who really can make a difference.

Such as former president Obama. He changed America. He made us LEGAL. It is a DISGRACE that it took the US this long for freaking marriage to become legal. That was only 5 YEARS AGO. And now we have a president who would be more than happy to overthrow all of it.

If we had more representation on social media, things may be different, better, and safer. Love, Simon was revolutionary, and is rated R21 is some countries! Unacceptable. We need more supporters, more representation. Sorry for the rant. Just the truth. We do not have enough representation."

Kelly (she/her), 14, Florida, lesbian, cis female

"I think there isn't, honestly. Most representation in the media of the LGBTQ+ community is either negative, not there at all, or the character gets killed off at some point. It's only now that the media is starting to portray, little by little, positive representation of the LGBTQ+ community. It's still not enough though. The LGBTQ+ community is still represented, most likely, almost the absolute least out of all, and I think that needs to be changed. We need more positive representation of the LGBTQ+ community in the media."

Day (she/her), 14, Illinois, ace/pansexual, female

How has social media helped/ hindered the LGBT+ community?

"I think it gives people who aren't out, or who aren't accepted by their friends or family, a sense of community. When someone is in a situation like that, it's important that they have some support and acceptance."

Ashton (he/him), 16, Michigan, gay, male

"Social media has helped the LGBT+ community by putting us out there. Before social media, some people thought it was wrong because they didn't really understand it. But after we got social media, the younger generations (us) learned that we need to tolerate each other more and become more aware that everyone is a person."

Cody (he/him), 15, Kentucky, gay, male

"For me, social media has been an outlet because I'm

not really out to my family and it helps with educating me more with the LGBT+ community.

But, there are also downsides to social media with people who come onto accounts just to be a bigot, looking for fights and all that such. I feel like social media helps more people stay informed on what's going on with anything and it helps a lot of 'troubled' teens and young adults who may be questioning or just need someone to talk to."

Charlie (they/them), 14, Florida, asexual panromantic, agender

"I feel that social media has hindered the LGBT+ community because there are so many harsh people in this world and with the social media, it's very easy for the hate to spread."

Richard (he/him), 16, Texas, gay, male

"I think social media is trying to help advance the LGBT+ community in such a wrong way that it's hindering us from politely correcting people. People get upset over the smallest thing like a newspaper article misgendering someone. It's not social media's

place to fight someone else's battles. I know misgendering isn't good, but articles do it for publicity and fighting over that article gives them what they want."

Carter (he/they), 16, Illinois, pansexual, trans masculine

"Social media has helped the LGBT+ community come together. We are able to communicate with one another from across countries and overseas. Most that are a part of the community now feel like we have a voice and at least a small platform that can stand as a safe space for others.

The 'phobias' of others against bi, pan, and trans people, along with other sexualities and genders is what is hindering the community. The close-minded people also feel they have a voice to hurt and manipulate people to feel the same way as them or at the least, people feel scared."

Maggie (he/them), 15, Kentucky, gay, agender

"As someone who lives in a small town, I don't see a lot of LGBT+ representation. We have about a total of

two out gay kids at our school so most kids don't even know what LGBT+ stands for. That's why I count on social media accounts so I can keep growing my knowledge on the community."

Avery (she/her), 15, Kansas, lesbian, female

"I think social media has helped the LGBT+ community in many ways. One being that social media helps show representation and another being that it has helped many LGBT+ people feel more comfortable and confident with themselves. It has helped many people, including myself, come out!"

Alex (she/her), 12, California, bisexual, female

"Social media helps the LGBT+ community because it puts information about it out there for people who have questions about it, or for people who think they might be in the LGBT+ community."

Nat (she/any), 14, Kentucky, bisexual, female

"Social media helped me find who I am. Before I got Instagram, I only knew what gay, bi and straight were.

When I started questioning my sexuality, I had figured I was bi. When I finally got Instagram, I discovered pansexual and thought that was a lot better. Over time, I started realizing I'm actually asexual panromantic.

Also, without social media, I would have never figured out I'm transgender. Before social media, I didn't even know what that was! Social media has definitely helped a lot."

Dakota (he/him), 16, Mississippi, asexual, trans male

"Social media has helped the LGBT+ community by providing us with a platform. It's an easier way to reach out and be heard. Media has helped many discover who they are within the community and has led to many movements. It allows us to create safe environments for ourselves and learn more about who we are.

Thanks to media, the LGBT+ community has grown in both population and support, but also in education of identities and sexualities."

Ashley (any pronouns), 18, Michigan, pansexual, genderfluid

"Social media has helped the LGBT+ community by connecting groups of LGBT+ members who would not normally interact. This has created a wonderful environment of love and support that is especially helpful for people who do not have support in their daily lives."

Fran (she/her), 15, Utah, biromantic asexual, female

"I think it's helped spread awareness and helped people understand that there is more than just 'gays' and that not all white people are gay. I feel like people are starting to accept LGBT+ more because people on social media are explaining how it is and love is love."

Breanna (she/her), 14, Washington, bi, female

"I believe that social media has helped the LGBTQIA+ community because it gives us all a place to find people just like ourselves. It is so hard finding people of this community because in the real world, a lot of people don't wear the name so proudly as they do on the internet. Here, we have a place to enlighten people and interact with people just like us. Though it does give homophobes a place to also voice their

opinions against us.

We are stronger in numbers. With Instagram and Twitter and Facebook, we have got places to get together and form a stronger community just by following someone or friending them, which is so much harder to do just walking down the street or going to school."

Allen (he/they), 15, North Carolina, pansexual/ asexual, trans male

"First of all, social media has brought people together. It has made people who are part of the LGBT+ community realize they aren't alone. We are just like everyone else. Social media has also helped by allowing us to plan large events, like pride parades or other supportive activities and fight for equality. Social media impacts the LGBT+ community by a lot."

Sarah (she/her), 15, California, lesbian, cis female

"The LGBTQA+ community has been closeted and when people join, we accept them right away! We don't say you're not good enough, we say, 'Welcome To The Family!'. We accept them! If they're closeted,

that's fine. We still love them! When they come out, we still love them and we still support them. When they come online, they feel safer because when they're in person with someone, they get scared they'll be mistreated. Online, they be themselves and express who they really are!"

Asher (he/him), 14, Florida, gay, polyamorous, trans male

"Social media has helped the LGBT+ community in the way that we have been able to gain support from others, in and out of our community. Not only that, but it has helped others gain knowledge about our community. All of this helps us to become a more diverse and accepting world."

Lionel (he/him), 16, Connecticut, asexual, trans male

"In my opinion, I think it spreads awareness that this is a topic people care about and can help others in the LGBT+ community. I like to try to create a space where people can realize they're not alone and others will fight with them against hate."

Leo (he/him), 15, Ohio, pansexual, male

"Social media has given LGBT+ people, who are closeted or can't come out at the moment, a safe space where they can be who they are, without being judged. They can also get advice on how to come out or how to withstand an unsafe environment."

Lilly (no pronouns), 13, Florida, homoflexible panromantic, female

"In my experience of being on online LGBT+ accounts, it seems like just about everyone on there is so open-minded and willing to do things like use your proper pronouns, even when sometimes at school and even your family won't. It's a way to find a group of people who respect you and just see you as any other human, who just happens not to be straight or cis. It creates a space where everyone is so willing to help everyone. It gives people a sense of community, where there might not have been one before.

It also gives people in the LGBT+ community a place where they can feel safe and don't have to worry about people judging or making fun of them."

Jasper (he/him), 14, Illinois, asexual panromantic, FTM

How easy is it telling different people about your sexuality/ gender?

"It's very hard to tell people about my sexuality and gender because it is very confusing; I am polyromantic, graysexual and genderfluid, which, are all quite complex. If I try to explain, I get told, 'That isn't a real thing,' or 'There's only 2 genders,' and sometimes I get the classic, 'All f*** go to hell' line.

Another thing about trying to explain it would be that I'm always questioning. I've changed my gender label so many times I can't count, and I have no idea what my sexuality is – I just label myself as gray/poly to make it simple, since it's not a huge change if I switch labels.

Overall, it is exceedingly hard to talk to people or explain it to people because the majority of the population is uneducated and ignorant on the topic."

Kade (he/they), 13, Delaware, polyromantic graysexual, genderfluid

"For me, it's actually easy explaining my sexuality. The way I've found works best, is to approach a person and tell them the depths of your sexual/ romantic preference(s) without first explaining the term(s). I am a demisexual, and pansexual transgender male. And, while it's usually easy explaining my sexuality, I rarely ever try going into detail about my gender, and just instead try to avoid it at all costs."

Xavier (he/him), 18, Georgia, demisexual/pansexual, transgender male

"I find that it's very hard to tell people how you identify with sexuality (and gender) in the beginning. But once I had told a couple of people, it had become much easier, and I also felt a lot more validated with who I was. After about the 100th time, it's so easy to just say something like, 'Oh, I'm bisexual' and not feel like you're telling this huge secret anymore.

Coming out was worth it, even if my mom doesn't believe me. But, remember to only come out when you think the time is right and when you feel safe."

Alayna (she/her), 15, Ohio, bisexual, woman

"So, I'm panromantic and non-binary. Telling people I'm pan is a bit hard because people are always saying, 'So you're bi?'. Sometimes I don't have the energy to fight them on it. When I do try to explain that it's not bi because bi is two genders and pan is all, you know, it usually turns into the 'There are only two genders' argument. By that point, I'm almost afraid to come out as non-binary because of the backlash that I got. My mom is sort of the only one that accepted it and asked questions respectfully."

Lily (she/they), 14, Maryland, panromantic, non-binary

"Well, it's not that easy to come out about your sexuality/gender because you never know how the person/people you are telling are going to react.

Basically, you have to get to know a person, and build up trust and respect from that person. And based on how they react, you could potentially lose that relationship you have with a person altogether, or a greater bond will form."

Ellen (she/her), 15, North Carolina, lesbian, female

"It's pretty easy because I don't give a damn what

people think about me or say about me. It's easier to tell guys, at least for me. I feel as if some girls will judge me and automatically assume I like them or something."

Courtney (she/her), 17, Wisconsin, bisexual, female

"I straight up yelled 'I am a flaming homosexual' in the middle of school; I think I'm fine. But if it was someone like my grandparents, it would be very difficult."

Leila (she/her), 14, California, lesbian, female

"My sexuality is easier than my gender. I am a proud pansexual, but I'm not sure on my gender. I prefer the name Mark to my birth name and I don't like being called a girl. I don't know, it's just difficult to tell the person even if they understand to call me Mark or call me by he/him pronouns. Because I feel like I don't deserve it? Or if I say, 'Oh yeah, I think I finally realize I'm trans' then I'm not... I feel like I'm lying."

Mark (unsure), 14, Alabama, pansexual, unsure

"I think it's actually very hard because some people

might just not agree with it or whatever, but some people will actually take it to a physical level. As a gay CHILD, that's scary and it makes me scared to, kind of, out myself."

Xitlali (they/he), 13, Arizona, lesbian, female

"For me, it's kind of hard telling people I'm gay because my father is a hardcore Republican, so obviously he has certain views on how people should live their lives. He says he doesn't have a problem with same-sex marriage, but he always makes jokes or off-handed comments about it. Plus, my grandmother thinks 'All gays will burn in hell' so that doesn't really help.

I know that when I tell them, they'll still love me, but I always have this feeling that it will be different."

Rose (she/her), 16, Massachusetts, gay, female

"I personally think that it's different for everybody, because some people are aware of their accepting friends and family. Some know that it's an unsafe topic to discuss. Others are just totally unsure of what people will think, which can be terrifying.

I personally had an easier time coming out to my friends and family since I already knew they were LGBT+ friendly. Other people don't have that advantage though."

Eva (she/they), 15, North Carolina, pansexual, genderfluid

"When people ask what gender you are, or even what sexuality you are, it can be uncomfortable. Depending on who you are as a person, you respond in many ways. From my prospective, it can be a little annoying. But on the other hand, you are letting people know how you feel and who you are as a person.

Going through my life, I've identified as many things from gender-neutral to agender. So answering this question, more than likely, it's going to change throughout a person's life until they find who they truly are.

Being in a world that is run by mostly hate and anger, being loved by people you feel in contact with is the most amazing feeling. In conclusion, be you and don't be scared to answer a simple question because, most likely, it'll turn out positive and you might even make a new friend!"

Charlie (they/them), 14, Pennsylvania, pansexual, non-binary

"In my experience, telling my family and friends my sexuality and gender was very horrifying...

It was a very stressful year for me and there were a lot of emotions! I was worried I would get kicked out of my house and people would beat me up or make fun of me, and some did. But, I learned to ignore it and just be who I am.

One of my inspirations was, and still is, Miles McKenna on YouTube. He taught me to be myself and not let anyone change that and to stay true to myself. I still haven't come out to some of my family that I'm pansexual and non-binary yet but that is okay!

You need to go at your own pace. You don't want to rush into things and feel really uncomfortable. You need to come out when you are ready. That is the most important thing about coming out! Maybe you can go to support groups for the LGBT+ community! I promise you that you will be accepted, loved, and cared for! No matter how tough it is, you will get through it – I promise!

People love you and they will always love you no matter what you do or who you are, they love you – always remember that!"

Ash (they/them), 13, Ohio, pansexual, non-binary

"It's sort of easy for me to tell people my sexuality and gender. There's a lot of people who it doesn't bother but some people have an issue with me being a lesbian. They try to hate on me for it but I just block them out because their opinion doesn't matter to me."

Jill (she/her), 17, Tennessee, lesbian, female

"For me, it's really easy. I'd rather them ask than assume, me being genderfluid. I actually like explaining it to people. Well, that's how I am. Other people may not be but yeah, that's how it is for me."

Alyssa (she/they/he), 15, Rhode Island, bisexual, genderfluid

"It all depends who the people are and how close they

are to you. If they're really your friends then they'll accept you no matter what and you'll feel comfortable telling them. If they're a stranger, it's easy because they didn't know the past you."

Kenny (he/him), 13, Tennessee, pan, male

"It's pretty easy to tell people that I am bisexual. I'm very open about it. When my peers ask me, I'll happily tell them but when an adult asks or says something, I'm hesitant or I sometimes lie about it. But, other than that, it's fine. I just get a little anxiety."

Sanai (she/her), 14, Pennsylvania, bisexual, female

"It's pretty easy for me to tell people about my sexuality if they're my age, just because I'm a pretty open person and I don't feel that it's something I need to hide, and I'm a bit more comfortable around kids my age. But, if it's an adult, I tend to be a little less open and act more 'hetero' because it's really hard to tell what their views are just by looking at them."

Abby (she/her), 15, Maryland, lesbian, female

"Coming out to different people can be really difficult, especially if it's someone close to you, such as a parent. Many parents will respond with, 'It's just a phase' or even, in some cases, kick them out in the streets. It can also be hard to come out (to a stranger/ people you've just met) when you don't fully trust someone, telling them a vulnerable thing, such as your sexuality or gender identity."

Alex (he/they), 14, Ohio, panromantic gray-asexual, demiboy

"It really depends on who the people are. If you're talking about it with people who are in the community, it's probably way easier than talking to someone outside of it. The queer community (for the most part) understands where you're coming from in a way that almost every cisgender and heterosexual person can't.

I first came out to my friends, who all happened to be queer. It was much harder for me to tell my family and peers. If I know that someone is in the queer community, it's easy for me to sit down and have an open conversation with them, even if they're a complete stranger, when I still haven't mustered enough courage to talk to my family, teachers, and other people about my identity."

N (they/them), 15, California, polyromantic ace, masc non-binary

"It's kind of hard to explain the whole genderfluid aspect to people. The gay part is easy. But when I try to tell them I'm genderfluid, they ask what it means and I tell them, 'Some days I feel like a boy and other days a girl. Some days neither and some days both'. But, for most people, they can't grasp the concept that you don't have to be one solid gender. Gender isn't just binaries, it isn't just male and female, it's how you label yourself. Your gender is how you perceive yourself."

Tyler (he/him), 15, Massachusetts, gay, genderfluid

"Well, for me, it started out being really hard, mostly because I didn't even want to accept it myself. It sucked because I wasn't letting myself be who I really was.

When I was in elementary school, I noticed I really liked being around girls… like a lot. But, I also realized that I had a bunch of crushes on boys. So I

just decided that I was just really friendly and since I had crushes on boys, I wasn't gonna question anything.

Then, middle school came and I started getting a different feeling towards my 'best friends'. But again, I still liked guys so I didn't question it. But then, towards the end of middle school, I realized how often I thought about girls… I honestly didn't know what I was because I only knew of 'gay' and 'straight'. So… I looked it up.

I took a bunch of BuzzFeed sexuality tests and all of them came back as 'bisexual'. I then went on to search and discover what being bisexual meant, and through this, I was beginning to accept myself as I was, and it felt like something had lifted off my chest. Then came the scary part… coming out…

I didn't really know what I was doing, for sure… I just knew I was scared. So, the first person I decided to tell was my best friend. Now, her family is pretty much the most homophobic, transphobic, and sexist I know. But me and her were extremely close and I knew she'd listen. So, I told her, just flat out said it while we were at dinner. She kinda looked at me and I looked back, and she said, 'Okay'. She then continued to eat.

That experience was so easy that I knew I could tell my mom with no problems. Now, I knew from the start that my mom wouldn't get mad or hate me, because we'd had talks when I was young about treating everyone the same. It took me a few months, but I finally did it. She looked at me, I looked back, and she said, 'Okay'. Now, I want you to understand how comforting hearing people say 'okay' to that is for me. Hearing that made me feel like it was just how it's always been, like nothing needed to change.

So, I told my dad. He was a little confused because he didn't know what being bi meant. After I explained it, he was fine and happy I told him.

Then, I decided the easiest thing to do… was to come out on Instagram. Everyone at my school and everyone I love follows me and always sees my posts. So I thought I'd knock 'em dead with one hit instead of fifty million over and over. So, I came out. Everyone was so so supportive of me. There were a few people who had problems with me afterwards but I didn't like them anyway.

So from then, it's one of the first things I tell people. I'm proud of who I am. No one can change that."

Dabria (she/her), 15, South Dakota, bisexual, female

"Telling people about my sexuality and gender is never easy. They can be the least homophobic or transphobic person in the world and I will still have a hard time. It's because we must be careful coming out. If you say something to the wrong person, you can be in danger. As scary as it is though, telling people about who you are can be one of the most freeing things in the world."

Emily (she/they), 14, Minnesota, pansexual, genderqueer

"Telling people about my sexuality is pretty difficult. Being bisexual, even members of the LGBT+ community sometimes say, 'Make a choice', 'You're just confused' etc. It doesn't bother me as much as it used to if that happens. I just say, 'Ha-ha F you too buddy' and move on with my life."

Rylee (she/her), 15, Texas, bisexual, female

"It depends who you are telling. I feel like if you're telling one of your best friends then it might be easier because they know you. But, telling your parents may be harder or maybe even impossible, especially if you know that they are not supportive of the LGBT+

community.

But, once you are out to many people, you start to become very open about yourself. You don't hide it as much. You start to act like yourself. You don't hide anymore. So, I say that it all depends on who you are telling."

Tricia (she/her), 15, California, lesbian, female

"Sometimes, I'm afraid of how people will react to hearing that I'm bisexual. People like to think what they like about you when they hear about you being bisexual. They think I'm confused, and that I will eventually pick one route or the other.

But I won't. I like girls, and I like boys and I am not ashamed of it. Going into high school, I decided to stop worrying about what people think of my sexuality. I'm more open about my bisexuality now, and even though it's terrifying every time I tell somebody new, I'm happier. I'm no longer keeping a part of myself hidden."

Jenna (she/her), 15, Texas, bisexual, female

"It's not easy telling people about my sexuality, especially when I'm unsure myself. People always think that once I say something, it means I've made up my mind, when in reality, I'm still questioning it. It's something I also want to be 100% sure with when I do figure it out, because when you grow up in a Hispanic household, it's something that is looked down on, or at least not approved of. I don't know if I'm straight, bi, or pan. I just know if I love someone or not. That's all that matters."

Coco (she/her), 16, Connecticut, questioning, female

"It depends on the person but usually, for me, it's hard. I have a lot of trouble talking to people normally, so it then escalates when it's something more personal."

Evelyn (she/they), 15, California, grey ace/pan, genderfluid

"Coming out to friends was sort of easy, because I knew they would support me no matter what. It's easier to come out to your peers, but adults are a whole different story. I've come out to a few teachers and they've been supportive, but it's still scary and I

find myself putting off coming out to other teachers because I'm worried about what they'll say, what they'll do, if they'll ask weird questions or if they'll try and get me in trouble.

Coming out to my parents was 10 times harder, because I was afraid of being judged or ridiculed or even yelled at for being the way I am. Even if parents are supportive, it's still terrifying to tell them you're not straight or cisgender. You can't always judge whether adults are supportive or not, because a lot of the time they're really good at hiding it."

Mark (he/him), 15, Ohio, panromantic, trans guy

"So, it really varies. Like, it was fairly easy with my friends because we're all queer as hell (we're like over half of the school's GSA), but with my parents and my cousin it was hard because they're not great with LGBT+ stuff and my parents are abusive. But, it went really well with my cousin. I've made a lot of friends because of it (is that weird?) but at the same time, I get bullied for it.

It's still really hard every time, no matter who I'm telling, even now, almost 3 years later from the first time I came out. Some people will just never understand and be able to accept it. While it sucks, I've come to terms with that fact. I'm just going to be who I know I am or watch me as I go.

Talking about it with some people, it's like talking to a 2 year old. And talking with others is even more near impossible. Sadly, not everyone will agree that I should have every right they do. People are different. It's what makes life interesting.

I wish I wouldn't have to speak out just to be heard to make a simple plead for equality, but in this society I do. Some people just don't know. I think we need to educate them so that they can open their minds. And some people are stubborn and don't care about anyone but themselves. I want those people to realize we will never shut up or sit down and be silenced. Time has been up for so long. I will never give in. I will keep fighting no matter what anyone says. You can't silence what needs to be said.

People will always treat me differently. I don't care. If I stand out, I might be seen. If I'm seen, maybe someone will listen. If someone listens, maybe something will change. If something changes, maybe I won't have to hide. If I don't have to hide, maybe equality will start being seen as normal to everyone. The more normal it is to us now, the fewer generations we will evolve into that will accept hate in any form. If we lose hate, then we can all feel normal.

We shouldn't have to fear walking down a street or into school ever again, just because we're 'different'. Differences are amazing. Don't hate people for them. Explain to yourselves why it's too much to ask that we all feel safe no matter where we are or who we are. Explain to me why you think hate is the right answer. It never has been and never will be. Love wins. Time's up. End hate. Me too. Be the generation that ends hatred!"

Logan (they/them), 15, Illinois, panromantic grey asexual, genderfluid

What reactions have you had when you told people about your sexuality/gender?

"When I told my friend that I had a girlfriend, she stopped talking to me and she's not that friendly to me anymore. When I told my other friend, she said that I should tell my mom and she kept trying to give me advice and saying stuff like, 'I can tell her for you'. I appreciate that she's trying to help but I wish she would calm down on the fully coming out part. A lot of my friends actually smiled and said, 'I'm so glad you told us!'."

Gia (she/her), 13, California, pansexual, female

"When I first came out, it was to my brother (accidentally). I was in 1st grade and I got a crush on a girl named Diana. Now, I was really young so I didn't even know what 'gay' meant. I just knew that I liked girls like I liked boys. I thought it was totally okay. But, he told me it wasn't. He said not to worry because he still loves me or whatever but other people might not be so nice so it's best to keep it a

secret. At least, until I was older. Fast forward a few years...

My parents were watching a movie that just so happened to have gay characters. They are really homophobic and were talking about how gross it was and that it was unnatural. I got upset and asked, 'Well... what if one of your kids was like that?' and they were like, 'Thank God we'll never have to find out'.

So, later that night, after a lot of thinking and crying and whatever, I went back and told them it made me feel uncomfortable when they talked like that because I was one of those people they hated...

My mom ended up crying and trying to convince me that it wasn't actually true. My dad got angry at me for making my mom cry. And my siblings were making fun of the whole thing. Needless to say, I was kinda scarred by that.

So now, I kinda just try to see a person's reaction to the mention of certain LGBT+ topics before officially coming out to them. For the most part (since my parents are religious homophobes), I don't come out to their friends because 9 times out of 10, they're just as unaccepting. Other than that, I don't feel the need to tell anyone unless they flat out ask. My straight siblings don't have to, so neither should I."

Zahra (they/them), 16, Tennessee, pan, non-binary

"I found out I was bisexual about three years ago. When I told my family, none of them believed me. Then, I told my friends and they were happy for me. After I moved last summer, I met new friends and told them. They are also happy for me."

Kaela (they/them), 18, Ohio, bisexual, genderfluid

"I would say that for me, coming out to people can go a multitude of ways. For my sexuality (bisexual), when I come out to friends, it usually goes either really good and they are very supportive or they kinda say, 'Oh okay, that's cool' and just kinda go on doing whatever they were before. Both are great reactions in my mind.

With people who I don't know that well, I either get the 'Oh okay, that's cool' reaction or I get a confused reaction e.g. 'What's that?', 'Wait, really?', stuff like that. I've gotten pretty used to it. And the thing is, I don't usually tell people myself anymore. Most of the time, people just overheard me making a joke about me being queer or something like that. I do this thing where if I hear someone say 'gay', I go over and just kinda say 'I heard my name'.

When it comes to my family, it's a little different. Most of my family is very religious; some of them are very homophobic. So far, I've only told my parents, two of my cousins (one is trans and queer as well), my grandmother, and my brother. They all had different reactions.

My mom was the first person I ever told about being bi. She was a little confused and stuff like that at first but she helped me figure out what to identify as and stuff like that. She still has questions and she is really coming around with it. My dad, he didn't really care when I first told him but he's made it clear he still loves me but he doesn't agree with it.

My cousins, the first one, she was just kinda like, 'Oh okay' and we didn't really talk about it a lot. With the second cousin, he was amazing, he immediately was just so supportive and he was like, 'It's so great to have someone else in the family just like me'. He means a lot to me.

With my grandmother, she was amazing. She

somehow already knew. She asked some questions and we talked through stuff and she was super supportive. She's very very religious, so it makes me happy that she was able to support me so much.

With my brother, he was amazing as well. I told him after I told my parents. He basically said it didn't matter to him and I should've told him first.

My gender identity is a different story. My friends are the most supportive people in my life. They all use my name most of the time. Most of them use my pronouns, they all refer to me as a boy or non-binary. Most of my friends are queer. I have some straight friends as well and they are really supportive.

With other people, they aren't so quick to support. Some of them are fine. But, a lot of others make a lot of really offensive jokes when it comes to that. They use 'gay' as an insult and make trans jokes and stuff like that. This one kid came up to me and said, 'Are you a trans?' really snobby-like. I was taking a test while this happened, like I don't even know this kid. This one kid does the whole, 'Oh I'm fine with lesbians but not gay men'. He fetishizes queer women and makes awful jokes and stuff like that. He called me 'it' the other day and he asked me, 'Are you gonna be a transvestite when you get older?'. But I just ignore him.

With my family, my mom, dad, and my cousin know and that's about it. My mom is how she is when she first found out about me being bi. My dad, we haven't talked about it at all because my mom told him. My mom and I went to my therapist and we're working it out and she's agreed to let me buy clothes in the guys' section.

My cousin however, he's the best. From the day I told him, he has used my name and pronouns. I do the same for him, but it sucks because we have to misgender each other around family and stuff like that. So, I usually just use 'they/them' around him when we are around the family. He does the same for me. It doesn't bother me because those are my pronouns after all. He/him or they/them are perfectly fine with me.

Basically, with both of my identities, I find it easier to tell people that I know will be okay with it. If someone is very religious, it makes it a bit harder for me but you never know how they are gonna react in the end."

Trevor (he/they), 14, Florida, bisexual, non-binary

"When I told people I was dating a girl, nobody really cared. They said, 'Ok, as long as you're happy'. But, my gender is kinda hard for people. I was born a girl but I'm very masculine and tend to act more like a guy. I get asked, 'Are you a boy or a girl?'. I'll just respond to them, 'I am who I am'."

Rae (he/they), 14, Florida, pansexual, N/A

"My first reaction was when I was talking to my mom and it slipped out that I was bi. She said, 'When did this happen?' and she is very accepting so it wasn't that bad."

Gabi (she/her), 14, Iowa, bi, female

"I've had many mixed reactions with my sexuality and gender. I came out when I had my first serious queer relationship and my entire family freaked out. They went into complete denial and refused to talk about it. It took them a while, but now, 3 years later, they are very accepting.

The situation with my gender, I just recently came out (about a year ago) and people haven't been okay with it. Since I'm only 17, I'm not allowed to physically transition because my legal guardian will not allow me to. I've been told it's a phase and being transgender isn't real, but I know who I am.

I've recently noticed small things; my sister posted me as her 'MCM' and my friends correct others on my pronouns."

Connor (he/him), 17, Texas, pansexual, non-binary

"I first told a small group of my female friends that I was bisexual. Their reactions were all pretty much the same. They told me that they had figured that I wasn't straight due to the amount of support I have towards the LGBTQ+ community. Then, I told my sister and she said that she also knew, for the same reason.

About a year later, I made some more friends and I was particularly close to one boy so I told him. He was very surprised but has supported me since the day I told him.

A little while later, I told another friend (over text) and he wrote me a very long paragraph expressing his support for me and how unfair it is that only LGBTQ+ people are expected to come out, so he came out as straight to me.

Most recently, I came out to another good friend and she responded with a simple, 'Cool, I'm bi too'. So, I've experienced only positive reactions to my coming out, which I am very thankful for."

Celeste (she/her), 14, Connecticut, bisexual, female

"So, I came out to my mom because my little brother kept saying I had a boyfriend during dinner. I yelled, 'I don't like boys, I like girls!' and she looked at me, dropped her fork and cried. She said, 'Damn it, your grandma was right'."

Gracie (she/they), 13, Washington, pan, gender-neutral

"The first time I came out as bisexual was to my friends who were together, one gay and one bi, and they both screamed and jumped up and hugged me. Everyone else just sort of nodded and moved on. I haven't told many people about being trans but I've only gotten positive results, nothing too outstanding that I can remember."

Skylar (he/him), 14, Iowa, bisexual, demiboy/trans masc

"Well, I'm cis (maybe) and pansexual, and when I tell people they always look at me like I'm crazy, just because they don't know what pansexuality is. Then, I have to explain what it is and they have one of two answers. The first and best one is, 'Okay, cool'. The next one is kinda the worst, 'There are only two genders, so you're bisexual'. And I just don't know what to say after that so I just shrug and never talk to them again."

Josie (she/they), 13, North Carolina, pansexual, questioning

"I'm pan, ace, and demi. I came out to my mom about my sexuality in 8th grade while looking through the yearbook with her and telling her which girls I thought were cute. She told me not to slap a label on myself, as well as suggesting not to date any girls while I'm in high school so I don't get bullied or hurt.

My dad, on the other hand, was totally cool with it, in which I was very surprised because he's a hardcore conservative. He doesn't know about my asexual side, but I'd assume he'd care even less than the pan part of me.

However, I did tell my mom about the asexual part. I

told her that sex sounded really, really horrible and disgusting and I hated even learning about it. She said that we could get my hormones checked and I started crying, because I knew she always wanted grandkids from me but I couldn't give her that. To this day, even though we've talked about it a little more and she's okay with it now, I still feel like a disappointment.

There's no way in hell I'm telling them that I'm a demigirl because there's no way in hell that they'd understand. I did tell my 3 best friends about it. One is non-binary, so they totally got it. Two is as straight as a ruler but she totally supports the LGBT+ community. She was super confused though. And Three is hella bi and knows about the spectrum so she supports me as well."

Em (she/them), 15, Wisconsin, pan/ace, demigirl

"I did not really get a big reaction except for my friends telling people they have a gay best friend and I'm gay. And I have not actually told my grannie because I think she knows but she's a little weird with all that so... she thinks it but does not know for sure."

Angel (she/her), 17, Ohio, gay, female

"People have told me how it was just a phase and that I haven't met the right guy yet. These were people that I thought were my friends."

Grace/Chris (she/he), 18, Georgia, lesbian, female/ genderfluid

"I'm asexual and panromantic. I haven't told all that many people, just some close friends and my parents. My friends took it very well, though I'm pretty sure they had no clue about what ace and panro were. My parents were a little surprised and asked a bunch of questions about what ace and panro meant, but they otherwise took it very well. Also now, my parents have started making bad gay puns since I came out, which is comforting, oddly enough."

Bee (she/her), 16, Virginia, asexual panromantic, cis female

"The reactions I had when I came out as trans and gay were mostly good. I was surrounded by caring and accepting people so pretty much everyone was ok with it and immediately started using the right pronouns and name for me.

One of my friends even started trying to get other gay guys to date me because I would always complain about being single so he said, 'Well now you have a new market! So many more people who might date you! Let's go!'. And then he dragged me around school looking for my potential boyfriend.

But, the only negative reactions I had were from my family, who still haven't accepted me but are slowly coming to."

Max (he/they), 16, Texas, gay, trans

"People took really well to me coming out. My mum was really happy for me and my dad is glad I can't get pregnant. I've only ever had a few people talk rubbish to me but I don't care what other people think. It's my life and LOVE IS LOVE."

Haleigh (unsure), 14, Illinois, pan/lesbian, female

"Coming out story: I told my mom I was trans in a bout of crying (I had just told her about my depression and other stuff) and she completely denied me being a transguy. She said if I were trans, she'd know, and that I was the girliest girl before I turned 9. Now, she's

forcing me to read the Bible. She was going to force me to go to church and confess and whatnot, but we compromised that I'd just read the Bible. I'm not even Christian?"

Owen (he/him), 15, Nevada, bisexual, transguy

"I'm trans and I'm basically out to everyone (because everyone I had been friends with, when I came out, thought it would be great to out me to everyone without asking about what I wanted). I used to be forced to go to a Christian church, although I'm not Christian, and it really messed me up.

One night, I was coming out of the church with my dad and I just started crying. Like UGLY crying all over the place. I told my dad outside of the house of God and he was actually pretty chill about it. My whole family thought I was gay already.

My mom's an alcoholic and I had to come out to her about 5 times because she was too drunk to remember the first four. When she was actually sober, she looked at me and just said... 'What's a transgender?'. It was extremely obnoxious.

Anyways, most of my friends were chill but a few

disowned me from everything and tried to ruin my life, but jokes on them, I already ruined it. The end."

Isaac (he/him), 15, Pennsylvania, gay, trans

"So, I am pansexual, and when I came out, I didn't tell people unless they asked. Most people didn't know what pansexual meant so they would ask if I have a boyfriend, I say, 'No, I have a girlfriend', and then they say, 'Oh, so you're gay?' and I tell them, 'No, I'm pansexual'. Then, they ask what that means and I tell them and they usually don't think that there is a difference between pansexual and bisexual, so they just call me bisexual and I have to correct them."

Aricca (she/her), 15, Arkansas, pansexual, female

"I've had some strange reactions. First of all, when I told my parents, they said that it's a phase and that I don't know what I'm talking about, although I predicted they would say that. I have a few LGBT+ friends. When I told my bisexual friend, she said, 'Oh okay.' (I used to identify as bisexual before too, but now I'm just fully gay). I also have a FTM transgender friend. When I told him, we were in school and he didn't want anyone to hear us, so he just responded

with:

'So… you're full cat now'. To be honest, that reaction was quite hilarious."

Julie (she/her), 14, Alabama, gay, female

"I came out to my mom with a coming out song by Ally something? At the end of the video, it says to give the person coming out a big bear hug. So, she came up behind me while I was doing the dishes and picked me up and swung me around."

Jonelle (she/her), 14, Indiana, pansexual, cis female

Have you ever experienced hate?

"I've definitely experienced hate before. The town I live in is very conservative; and most people that live there are either incredibly religious or just plain hateful towards anybody not of the straight white male 'community'. Of course it's not all of them. A good fraction of them have a very open mind, but the majority aren't too LGBT+ friendly.

I moved to the town late last year, and the first school activity I went to was a football game. I went with one of the few friends I had already made, and it didn't end well. A boy was being incredibly rude to a girl I barely knew at the time. So, me, being one to not tolerate bullies, told the guy to bug off. He then retorted to calling me many many slurs and names. At the time, I wasn't completely comfortable with myself, so this was a pretty traumatic thing. The town I'd lived in prior never would have even considered hating on someone for their differences. The kicker of this is that, at the time, nobody knew I was even questioning.

Anyway, so after the slurs and the harassment, I basically had a mental breakdown. If this were to happen today, I would have just brushed it off and told him to kiss my b****. But then, I was incredibly sensitive to the idea. It seems like it wasn't a big deal, but even little things like that can really really put a damper on my self-esteem. This has happened multiple times since then, actually. Not with the same boy, but with a range of a lot of people just hating me for loving someone. How messed up is that?"

Jay (any pronouns), 14, Missouri, lesbian, female

"I've experienced hate in my family since I grew up in a religious family. I was always getting words thrown at me for being who I am. In school, I'm fine since I have surrounded myself with friends who accept me for who I am."

Misha (they/them), 15, Massachusetts, queer, non-binary

"It's not really as bad as it seems and I realize that now. But, during ninth grade, I had this best friend who had gone to a different school than I did and I believe she started to go her own way. I think when I

came out to her, it kind of affected her that way and stuff but I didn't know this. So it kind of hurt me. I guess you could say she was silently hating me and she never really talked to me all of that year and, even now, we still don't talk.

And I feel as though there are some people who think I'm weird because of my sexuality at school and it kind of drives them away from me. But other than that, no one really knows because no one really knows me for me, if you get what I'm saying."

Montana (she/her), 15, Maryland, bisexual, female

"Pretty much, just overhearing people being homophobic in classes or friend groups. Also, people saying that bisexuality isn't a real thing."

Naia (she/her), 16, Oregon, bisexual, girl

"Everyone's experienced hate. I know I'm not special when I say that I have received hate. Some have received hate from the start, some more recently. I can't say that I have experienced hate any greater than someone else, but I have received some.

The strongest and worst time was in fifth grade. I had been a boisterous child and hadn't really grown into myself yet. Basically, I was friends with this boy, and this girl (we'll call her Sally) was madly in love and was jealous.

Sally was tall, I couldn't relate. She was a lot bigger than me and was popular. Me being me, I was not, and was just seen as someone that was there. Everyone knew me, but nobody KNEW me. She bullied me and nobody really cared. So I did the only thing I thought I could do; I blocked everything out. In retrospect, this wasn't a good idea at all. I bottled everything up and struggled to feel things.

It took me weeks to realize that I had fallen in love with my current boyfriend (he's bi, I'm pan). I just sought happiness with a friend, and Sally couldn't really do anything about it. So, while my story might not be all that grand or dramatic, it still hurt and was the first major time I received hate."

Suzy (she/her), 13, Ohio, pan, demigirl

"It was in 7th grade that sticks out to me most. But, I came out as pansexual to a few of my friends and they told other people without me, so they started

making fun of me. I lost about 3 friends as well."

Yuugi (he/him), 14, West Virginia, pansexual, trans male

"I have experienced hate. When I first came out, most of my friends stopped talking to me. My mother turned away, and people I knew were shocked. I was used to getting hate from random people just because I was gay. It didn't make sense to me. But over time, people became less hateful and more understanding. For the ones who didn't, I'd just ignore them. I've realized you shouldn't change yourself for those who hate on you."

Vida (she/her), 14, New York, lesbian, female

"The first time I knew someone hated me was when I told the girl I thought was my best friend, in middle school, that I liked girls and boys. She stopped speaking to me that day and avoided me at all costs from then on. I still haven't come out to everyone, my mother included, because I am terrified of their reactions.

I am an avid Christian, but I firmly believe that the line in Leviticus, about men laying with men, is actually talking about pedophilia. It was a very horrible reality during the Roman Empire and Leviticus has been translated many times and child/man are very similar words in many languages.

Anyways, I have also experienced rejection from some other people who I have come out to. The fear of the whole situation chips away at my heart every day.

But, one day, I hope to find the best person for me no matter their gender identity or no gender identity."

Aileena (she/her), 16, North Carolina, bisexual, cisgender female

"Yes, I have experienced hate from my own family and friends and strangers for my sexuality and gender identity. It was verbal mostly, them saying that I have to be a girl because that's what I was born as, or I can't be non-binary and that pansexuality isn't real and I'm too young to know. Common stuff but it still hurts like hell."

Alex (they/he), 14, Utah, pansexual, demiboy

"Hate in itself is more complex than we tend to think at first. To say that you hate someone is to openly express that you have a strong emotion about that person, something that practically goes against the very nature of hate. As an already abstract idea, perhaps any 'hate' we have experienced was something entirely different.

That being said, it would be almost impossible for someone living in today's society to have not experienced hate in one way or another. I don't believe that I've ever directly experienced hate in relation to my sexual orientation, though most people just don't understand in the first place. I've certainly heard others make fun of or compare two completely different orientations, but that's kind of whatever.

The only real hate I've seen or heard of was said in, what I assume to be, ignorant jest, or people who truthfully thought it but were too afraid to say anything until they were hidden behind a computer screen. To anyone who takes time out of their own day to attempt to bring someone down, I would say that first and foremost, stop.

And secondly, in hindsight, we only have one life to live (regardless of whether or not you believe in reincarnation, this is our only shot in THIS life), so do you really want to spend it by bringing other people down?

Why not do something that helps other people, or something that you enjoy, so long as it doesn't hurt anyone else? And to anyone who has experienced hate, try not to wallow in it, it's not going to change anyone around you, the only thing you can change is yourself and your perspective."

Sacha (any pronouns), 15, Kentucky, panromantic demisexual, female

"I've experienced hate throughout my whole life for my weight and other things that I prefer not to say. It was one of the worst times of my life. The hate kinda ended in high school but you know how there's always that one chunk that's just gonna mess with people. It's been a hard journey trying to recover but I've finally learned to love myself for who I am."

Emily (she/her), 17, Texas, bisexual, female

"I have experienced hate. Yes, we all think hate is such a strong word, but it can definitely describe how some are treated. My boyfriend recently came out to

me as bisexual, and I received hate for standing with him, and staying with him. People hated me for trying to defend him when he was locked in a football locker, and he called me, sobbing. The words he said to me will never leave my head: 'They locked me in a locker… I don't know when I can get out… can you help me?'. He strengthened my resolve, and made me realize that yes, hate is terrible.

I was called s**** and s*** for dating someone who was bi and therefore might 'cheat' on me. He has never done any such thing, and I don't believe he ever will. Hate, though it hurt while it happened, brought us together."

Dyllan (they/them), 16, Massachusetts, panromantic demisexual, non-binary

"Ah, well yeah, I've experienced a lot of hate for who I am, pan, non-binary. People have said awful things that shouldn't be said to anybody (unless you're Donald Trump, sorry)."

Sam (they/them), 14, California, pansexual, non-binary

"Yes, most of my family and church are extremely anti-LGBTQ+ anything. It makes it very tough for me and the only time I can really talk to any of my family is when my sister is around, because she is a lesbian and understands what I'm going through.

My mom is constantly saying homophobic stuff and I can't say anything or I will be 'that child' that everyone dislikes and is awkward around. It is extremely hard for me and the biggest thing that makes it bearable is some of my friends at school. They help me find out what I identify as and are really great people."

Jackie (they/them), 14, Arizona, pansexual aromantic, genderfluid

"I experience hate all the time, even within the community. Usually, it's just some random person that goes through the SAGA (Sexuality and Gender Acceptance) community tags that comments that gay marriage shouldn't be allowed or there are no such things as bigenders, asexuals etc. There are also people in the LGBT+ community that believe that there are only two genders. I know it's hard to believe, but some members only believe in the L, the B, the G, and the T.

Those people are easy to handle because they're online. You can try to talk to them and ask them to not do the things they're doing, and if they are still bothering you, they can be blocked.

There are also people in my life that give me hate. Family members tease me and friends start to hate. It's a major problem for me when the people I love don't accept me. It's harder to deal with them because I see them in my everyday life and there is no block button for a human that speaks to you face-to-face."

Ash (he/him), 15, California, omnisexual & grey ace/demisexual, trans male

"The first time I ever experienced hate was about 2 years ago. In 2016, I came out as bisexual to my parents. They took it ok, but then told my aunts and uncles. Easter was coming up and I dreaded it because I didn't know if they would approach me. I was terrified! When Easter finally came up, it was my uncle that stared at me as soon as I got there. He confronted me and started yelling at me because he is super religious and it was embarrassing to have a gay in his house, and he asked my parents and I to leave, but his wife luckily took me in the other room and said that she was very proud of me being me no

matter what.

Even though it was a terrible experience, I still knew that some people wouldn't agree with me, but the people that do… they're the ones that deserve to be in my life!"

Marrissa (she/her), 15, Iowa, bisexual, female

"I mean yeah, I think everyone has experienced hate. Hate is what makes people who they are. You either get stronger and spread love, or you get weaker and create more hate.

I myself have experienced enough hate that most people would just kill themselves, believe me, I've thought about it. You can get hate from anything: being too fat, skinny, tall, short. I'm short and gay and my parents give me the most hate. Growing up, all I was ever told was, 'You're worthless', 'You're a b****' etc.

Most of that was from the people who I thought were there to love me the most. I'm not even out to them and they still hate me. I would rather be adopted and hated because then it wouldn't be my real parents hating me.

I have always been bullied at school and had kids be so rude. I have always had a really hard time making friends. Eventually, all the friends I thought I could trust stabbed me in the back and left me alone crying. All but a few.

All I have ever wanted is love and to be normal. There is no normal. Normal is a made-up word for people in power to use to put people down. Society created normal, but society isn't real. It's something everyone and no one made up. It's completely stupid. To use something so horrible to spread hate everywhere. To make people hate themselves. Why would anyone do that? To feel like they are better than everyone else?

The most hated thing is love. But why? The thing we all come from is the thing that gets the most hate? The thing that makes us happy. Whole even. Yet some people can't stand that. They take others' love from them. What do they get out of being so evil?

I guess there are some questions that can't or won't be answered. Maybe it's time for the world to pull their heads out of their a**** and realize there are a lot of people on this Earth who go unloved. Instead of hating them, realize you could be them. Love them.

At the end of the day, we all die. Why be greedy when

you can give that money to people who need it? When you die, you won't be needing that money. There are enough resources to fix the world. So, why not give it a try? Who knows… you might actually like spreading love and not hate."

Dylan (they/he/she), 14, Colorado, pansexual, genderfluid

What do you say to the haters?

"Personally, I either try to explain to them whatever it is that's bothering them because sometimes they're just ignorant. If I know that they're just trying to get to me by saying stupid stuff about my gender identity (I'm a trans male) or sexuality (I'm pansexual), then I just ignore it. Because in the end, I know I'm valid and I have bigger issues to deal with than a bunch of idiots I barely know saying hurtful things."

Ryan (he/him), 14, Connecticut, pansexual, trans male

"What do I say to the haters? It really depends. If it's someone who is just uneducated and is asking a question, I'm always willing to answer because ignoring them doesn't help me, them, or anyone else in the LGBTQ+ community.

If it's someone saying stuff like, 'haha lol that's so gay' or 'you f**', I'll tend to nicely explain why it's wrong because most people don't know better.

If it's someone who continues to pester me, or say, 'f**' or 'that's gay' when I'm around, I'll try to ignore them for a bit, but if they don't stop, I will haul off. My school doesn't do stuff to help and I tend to get a temper. I will yell at them and let them hear it. I know it's wrong to make someone hurt, but I only do it in extreme cases."

Breanna (she/her), 15, Indiana/Ohio, pansexual, female

"I would say F you, laugh in their face and ask, 'Is that all you have to say?' but I don't. I think it's just better to leave the peace."

Sammey (he/him), 15, Maryland, pansexual, male

"Nothing, you just hold your head up, kiss your boyfriend/girlfriend or ef and flip them off while walking past them."

Annabel (she/they), 14, California, omniromantic grey-ace homosexual, demigirl

"Hello to the haters. I usually just ignore them

because if they hate on me, they don't matter in my life."

Xander (he/him), 15, New Jersey, straight, male (trans)

"It really all depends on what they say.

*One response that never fails is to just walk away. Say 's**** you' in your mind and let them be. If the homophobes and transphobes are really bugging you then give them a piece of your mind. Let them have it. Hit them with the hard facts, such as: being gay is not a sin.*

God told the people that they didn't have to love the same gender to show their love for him. God never said that it was a sin or that it shouldn't be done. Also, if I am correct, does it not state that above all, you should love others, because love conquers over a multitude of sins?

*It's not being 'homophobic', because they aren't afraid, they're just a*******. By judging people for who they love, they have proven themselves worse than the people they are judging. Keep these things in mind next time you're called a 'f*****' (I hate that word)* *or 'gay' is used as an insult.*

If someone calls you 'gay' as an insult, they are homophobic, and if you take it as an insult, you're homophobic as well."

Charity (she/her), 14, Texas, questioning, questioning

"Well, let me start by telling you, don't let the hate of people get to you. Yes, I have expressed a lot of hate with family/friends not accepting me, and I honestly went through a really bad depression. One of the things I have learned so much more is, life is about finding yourself and if family and/or others do not accept you, do they really deserve you?"

Maddie (she/her), 16, Tennessee, unsure, girl

"To the haters:

'I wish I had said that she has always been stronger than you. I wish I had said that she has always been better than you. I wish I had said that I had more on my mind than you. I wish I had said that I was proud of who I am. I wish I had said that I was more persistent than you. I wish I had told you exactly who I

was in no uncertain terms. But I didn't. Now I will, but for some it's too late. She will never be able to prove her strength, but I know. And I guess that's enough.

That doesn't mean I'm going to leave it at that. No, I'm going to fight like hell in her name, and in mine. I'm going to fight until you realize why you are wrong, and correct your actions. I'm going to fight in the memory of all those who didn't make it. And I will persevere. There's no destroying me. I have too many names in my mind, too many emotions in my heart to stop fighting. I will fight until my dying day to pave a better road for those who follow me.'"

August (they/them), 16, Oregon, ace aro, agender

"Well, what I'll say to the haters is don't hate on someone just because you want to. Hate is a strong word for certain things and I don't really like that word. But why? It's because I have been hated before and it's not good because then the person will look at you bad and start rumors that won't be true. Plus, when you hate someone so much, you'll try bringing that person down and it's not right for us because we are all human and deserve to be respected like humans, no matter what color or what race or whatever you want to be.

Hate isn't a really good word to use because people will take it offensively and some people could take it as a joke, but it's not a word that should be used against a person. The word is kinda like a bully word and it's just not right for people to be using it if they're gonna bully someone.

But, what I'll probably say to the haters is don't hate on someone just because you don't like them, or don't hate on other people if you don't know what they have gone through."

Salma (she/her), 14, California, lesbian, female

"What I would say to the haters, 'I respect your opinion, but you do not have to be rude about it. If you do not like my art, writing, Instagram account, etc. then you can leave a respectful and helpful comment on how I could improve. If you are being rude just to be rude, I suggest you leave.'"

Max (he/they), 12, USA, pansexual, transgender male

"Why the LGBT+ community would benefit us:

In my opinion, I just think that it could help us accept

differences better. People like different things! And while we have a different opinion on those things, it's not our place to judge. I think the more diverse our community is, the more that people will come to accept it!

In my school, kids found out I was pansexual. And they didn't really like me for that. But as time moved on, people have come to terms with it. While they still have their opinions, we all accept it.

People need to learn that, no matter who you are or what you do, you don't stop us or anyone else from liking who or what we/they like. And that's that. And if you don't like it, that's okay! Everyone should still respect your opinion. And that's what matters. Everyone respects everyone! That's what I think matters. That everyone is happy and equal."

Dee (she/they), 14, North Carolina, pansexual, female

"To the haters, I say, 'Why does it matter if I like a boy or a girl? Or anyone other than the opposite gender? If I'm happy, that's all that matters. And if you don't like it then ignore me. I'm not changing myself just so a loser like you can like me'.

Then, I walk away."

Julia (she/her), 15, New York, pansexual, girl

"We are very friendly. We know what it's like to feel like you don't belong and since we hate that feeling, we wanna make sure that no one else feels that way. We are very kind to everyone, even if they hate the LGBTQ+ community. We just wanna be friendly and considerate to all those around us. We never wanna make anyone feel the way we do with all our criticism. We don't let the haters get to us because we know that, one day, they will see how friendly we are."

Josephina (she/her), 14, Kansas, bisexual, girl

What is it like attending a pride event?

"Honestly, it's kind of magical. You enter this area of people like you. People that have faced what you've faced with being LGBT+, people that are just more loving and caring. Everyone around you wants the same thing; that is equality. Through that, you make friends, and become a happier person.

Being at a pride event is like being at the zoo, except you're one of the animals in a cage, but you're harmless, all you want is to be free. One day the gate breaks, and you run for the exit. You'll do anything to be a free, harmless, animal. That's what pride's like. The gate is what's holding us back from being equal. When that gate breaks, we march our way out and into society."

Jackie (they/she), 14, California, panromantic, non-binary

"Each time I attend a conference or a pride parade, it is so inspiring and motivational. Everywhere I look I

see a confident human showing the world their true self. Sometimes, I feel so alone in my little town or looking at the media, like no one in the world is going to understand me. But being at pride is a way to show who I truly am, and have so much fun at the same time!"

Noah (he/him), 13, Massachusetts, gay, transgender

"This year was the first year that I ever went to pride. I remember crying on the way there because I never thought that I would get to this point. Once I got in, it was like a wave of joy had washed over me. People asked me my preferred pronouns and sexuality as if it was nothing. It made me feel very happy. My best friend had gone with me and she supported me the whole time. She even came out as bisexual that day! There was a drag queen show, Britney Spears was playing and everyone had a good time.

If you can afford it and it's safe for you, I really hope you would go to pride fest because it's the best feeling you could ever have."

Rowan (he/him), 14, Pennsylvania, pansexual, transgender

"It's extremely magical! You get to see more and more people who are like you and you feel valid while there! It's like seeing a family member you haven't seen in years."

Xitlali (they/he), 13, Arizona, lesbian, female

"It's honestly such an amazing experience. Seeing and meeting people that are proud of who they are and everyone is there expressing themselves. It was a really fun time. I went with friends and family and everyone was so accepting of me and one another."

Abi (she/her), 13, Tennessee, pansexual, cis female

"It's so surreal, honestly. It's like you're being surrounded with love and support, and it can be great if you haven't felt any in the past. You just see people who are 100% truly being themselves with no regret or fear. The diversity is tremendous too, at least in Hollywood. It was a day where I felt accepted and free, and I can't wait to go again."

Theo (he/him), 13, California, unsure, trans male

"Going to a pride event, for me anyway, can give you the best feeling and really make you come out of your shell. Like typically I'm really antisocial and just kind of try to keep to myself all the time, but when I was there, in the middle of a crowd of people there were some of the most interesting kind people I've seen; it just fills you with this positive energy that, when you feel it, you can't help but smile.

Though yes, there can be a point somewhere in there where you start to realize that your wonderful time is starting to come to an end and you get depressed, but there is always someone that will make you smile again."

Sean (he/him), 17, California, pansexual, guy

"It was really nice because there was representation for everyone out there and I learned a lot about gender identity and other sexualities. I got to talk to people who have gone through coming out and I got to hear the different ways that they have come out. Overall, it was a really cool experience."

Rhiannon (she/they), 13, Nevada, lesbian, agender

"It's like being inside a warm, kind, welcoming old lady's home with rainbow everything… including the cookies (*wink*)."

Cheyenne (she/her), 14, New Hampshire, bisexual, female

"It is magical. There is no other place, at least for me, to be around a family of queer people. To see everyone of different gender identities and sexualities coming together to spread love and rejoice in who we are; is more inspiring and heart-warming than anything else I've experienced.

This was my first year attending pride and I cannot begin to tell you how much it's helped me. Seeing all these happy, beautiful LGBTQ+ people all smiling and singing... I will never forget it. I danced with strangers and sang my heart out alongside some of the strongest people I've ever been around. We all shared a bond that can't be found anywhere else. We held hands and told each other to stay strong. It's an experience like no other. I felt like I could safely be myself for once in my life. It was wonderful."

Bryce (she/her), 18, Indiana, lesbian/queer, female

How can we strive for equality?

"We can strive for equality by reminding people that if they wouldn't want it said to them, they shouldn't say it at all. If they remember that, it would make a difference. If they would do what they do and say what they say to a child then where is the humanity? Sometimes people need reminders to be decent. Just like mother has always said, 'Give Respect, Get Respect'.

People need to know safety to be able to accept. Part of inequality is ignorance. If you eliminate ignorance on the subject, it would become more clear."

Carrie (they/them), 18, Connecticut, bisexual, genderfluid

"We can strive for equality by learning to first, accept all of the identities within our community. There is a lot of prejudice against other sexualities and/or gender identities in the LGBTQ+ community. We need to learn to respect all of the letters and embrace the '+'.

Once we do this, we will be unstoppable because we will then all treat each other equally and won't be fighting battles with each other, and focus on winning battles against those who shut us down."

Trevor (he/they), 14, Florida, bisexual, non-binary

"The matter of fact is that racism is due to ignorance. Ignorance is bliss in some ways, and not in others, but in order for people to change their mindsets on whatever stereotypes they may have, they have to be willing and open-minded to change. Sometimes, there is a severe type of stupidity that doesn't seem to have a cure, so patience is required for change to occur."

Lucas (he/him), 16, California, pansexual, male

"How can we strive for equality? We have to first accept that gender is a spectrum, only then can we reach a point where our society has matured enough to be equal."

Nova (she/her), 16, Massachusetts, pansexual, female

"Equality? I think we need to change the world entirely to have total equality among all people. Raise better, more open-minded and loving generations. Find new ways to show how everyone is equal."

Em (they/them), 15, Connecticut, pansexual polyromantic, genderfluid

"I think everyone should try to just be accepting. If everyone has a mindset of acceptance then they can understand that people, who are different from them, are no less of human beings, and give us the same human rights as themselves."

Jamie (they/he), 15, Michigan, pansexual, masculine non-binary

"We can strive for equality by being around people who accept us for who we are and cut out the people in our lives that don't. We have to stick together and fight (peacefully) to make a difference!"

Miles (he/they), 13, Virginia, queer, trans/non-binary

"I think of it more as how we can save equality. At this

point, we are going back in terms of progress, and even though nobody says it outright, we are subliminally telling people that they are less important based on their race or sexuality. One major way we can stop this is by talking to the people who protest signs telling people it's okay to be their race. We can also try to get rid of phobias (heterophobia, homophobia), maybe by exposing the people with the phobia to the thing they are scared of."

Joey (they/them), 16, Texas, pansexual, other

"How can we strive for equality? A lot of ways. Not everyone is treated fairly when everyone should be; it may bother you to see a gay couple, but suck it up. I'm gay and seeing a hetero couple bothers me a bit, but I don't protest them and how they feel. And I hate it when people think you'd date anyone gay. I mean, thanks for the offer, but I don't find random straight people and ask if you'd date them.

And African-Americans, just because they have a certain skin color and some people act differently doesn't mean you can interpret the whole race as that. Most black people are nice and caring and also, trans isn't a mental disorder and it's not hard to explain to children. You want to have the body of the opposite sex? So what? You wanting to do that shouldn't bother everyone around you.

I hope one day everyone can live in peace and not be bothered by race, religion, color, creed or sexual orientation."

Dillon (he/him), 13, Massachusetts, gay, cis male

"We can be more open to the idea that everyone is welcome into this world without anyone judging them. Equality is very important, no matter who you are."

Emma (he/she), 13, North Carolina, bisexual, genderfluid

"We can strive for equality by being accepting and kind. If you see boys dressing as girls or girls dressing as boys, support them. If you hear someone saying something rude about another race or gender, you need to tell them what they are saying is not ok, even if people make fun of you for saying it. Just be supportive and kind to all people of any race, gender, or sexual orientation."

Hayden (he/him), 15, New York, bisexual, male

"I think we can strive for equality by teaching people how to treat others and make harsher rules for hate crimes so people will be less likely to commit them. Another way is to teach people to treat others well in early education so they know how to treat others later in life. A final way is making people who treat minorities poorly outcasts in regular society."

Kai (he/she/they), 16, Missouri, pansexual, pangender

"We can strive for equality by respecting one another. I don't expect people to understand, but I just want you to know that I am who I am and you can't change that.

I didn't start our LGBT+ page so that we can just be another account on Instagram. I started it so that it can become a place for people to learn about the genders and sexualities. If they don't want to learn, that's ok, they just need to understand that we can't just go away. We are here to stay and we will be heard.

I understand that our government is meant to move slowly. But moving so slowly that people have been marching for LGBT+ rights since before there were color televisions is unacceptable. We need to work on people respecting us, because respect is the first step towards equality."

Parker (he/him), 15, California, pansexual, FTM boy

"We can strive for equality by everyone treating each other the same, regardless of differences. This includes respecting people's opinions verbally and mentally. You don't have to agree with them to respect their opinion. Equality is achieved when we treat everyone the same way."

Luna (she/her), 17, Arkansas, bisexual, trans female

"Although it might seem to take forever, it has the capability of eventually being reached. A realistic definition would be that we all have the same chances of fairness to whatever we do. To be treated equally is the goal, and to have that happen, first, we would have to accept EVERYTHING as it is and go from there.

Religion seems to be a big factored thing that keeps us from seeing over certain things. Though every religion has rules and regulations to go by, they are simply guidelines to go by. To eliminate the unfair idea that you must judge and treat others who may go against what your beliefs are differently would be a great starting point.

Everyone simply cannot share the same opinion(s), but we can look past them and stand together on the facts, things that can be proven true or false, unlike an opinion. Together, equality can happen."

Kenna (she/her), 15, Mississippi, lesbian, female

"I'm a firm believer that the only road to equality of marginalized groups is through education and representation. What we teach in schools and what we see on screens, at least where I'm from, seems to be catering towards bigots in an effort to make them feel comfortable. In reality, the only way to change is to feel uncomfortable enough to re-evaluate your opinions. Sex ed and just regular classes for young children need to expose them to the fact that LGBTQ+ people exist and that's okay.

A generation of open minds is the generation that will bring change."

Zahavah (changes/they/them), 16, Connecticut, bisexual, genderfluid

Other?

Gaydar

"Well for me, I just feel like with some people, I can just tell about them. But, this does not go for everyone. I can tell by how people dress sometimes if they are very open about it, but see nowadays, it's not that easy because clothes don't really show who you are unless it says something like, 'Hey, I'm gay' or something like that. But yeah, for me it's kind of easy but it kind of is not at the same time."

Tricia (she/her), 15, California, lesbian, female

Gender pronouns

"Gender is completely fluid. Some people may identify as cisgender for their entire life; others may change who they identify as every other day. He and Him pronouns are ones that belong to someone who identifies as male, while She and Her are designated to females.

Beyond the binary is when pronouns become more

complex. Most non-binary people use the singular form on They and Them; others choose to use newer ones, such as Xe or Xem. It is never rude to politely ask someone what their pronouns are, even if they are cis.

In modern times, it is slowly becoming part of meeting someone for the first time. For example, a conversation may follow like this, 'Hi, I'm George, he/ him, how are you?'. While this may take some time to become integrated into social norms, it will help transgender children become more comfortable with who they are and more accepted."

Lynn (she/they), 15, Washington, lesbian, female demigender

Advice

"My best advice for coming out is not to overthink it. I've come out to my friends but not my family yet, and my friends don't look at me any differently. I'm waiting to come out to my parents until I know for certain I'll have a safe place to go if they ask me to leave, but I doubt they'll look at me any differently as well. If you plan on coming out, whether it be to your friends or family, make sure you have a safe place to go in case

things don't go to plan, and surround yourself with people that will support you."

Emily (she/they), 15, Wisconsin, pansexual, female

"Today is not worth your tears. Life is hard but you must be strong. There are people who need you, and that little voice in your head telling you that there is no one is wrong. You're beautiful, don't let the negative ugliness define your beauty. You must break free. It may be hard but life can be whatever you want it to be.

You want to be happy, you must change everything to find it. It's like a maze that's constantly changing, you can't look at it straight forward and with negativity, you must look above and plan; you have to be positive.

There is so much beauty in the world yet so many are blinded by the ugliness; don't, be blinded. You are too smart and brave and everyone knows it. The people that bring you down are just obstacles you will get around. Life will get better if you believe and make it better.

Your life is your own to mold. When you get frustrated, you don't throw the clay away; you smoosh it all down and you start again and this time it will be better."

Dylan (they/he/she), 14, Colorado, pansexual, genderfluid